Medieval Woodcarvings

Of

Ripon Cathedral

choir stalls, canopies,

ceiling bosses

and misericords

BY

Maurice H. Taylor

And

Derek Ching

Contents

Contents Page

Preface

People come to Ripon Cathedral for different reasons and, as such, they engage with at least one of three considerations. What are those three?

First, there is the sheer beauty of the building which encompasses both bold architecture and intricate detail. Second, there is the unfolding of history illustrated by specific monuments as well as by the evolution of the building through successive generations of construction. Third, there is spirituality because a Cathedral, unlike other historic houses, is a place not only of Christian tradition but also of living faith.

Beauty... History... Spirituality...

All these three considerations are in fact brought together when you view the medieval woodcarvings and misericords. Each undoubtedly represents beauty; each offers either a glimpse of ecclesiastical and biblical history; each takes us into the realm of spirituality – our relationship with God.

It is for this reason amongst many that I commend this book to you and pay tribute to Maurice Taylor and Derek Ching the authors, as well as to the Friends of Ripon Cathedral and all who have made its publication possible. In reading it you will be able to piece together the story of how the carvings came into being, who was responsible for doing them and you will learn something of the story of faith which underpins them. The photographs will inspire and encourage you either before or long after your visit.

As Dean of Ripon I, with my other senior colleagues, have the custody and stewardship of this fine building. Personally, I describe it as one of those places that reveals something new about itself every time you enter. The woodcarvings alone are testimony to this fact. Even a lifetime of visits would not satisfy a keen mind but at least this book gives us a considerable insight into the richness of what we can all too easily take for granted.

Keith Jukes – Dean of Ripon - 2009

The Authors

Maurice H. Taylor, BA, Cert. Ed., MA, since retiring as a head of school in Leeds, has been involved in many projects researching the history of the Ripon area, its buildings and its people. He frequently lectures and leads guided walks with titles as diverse as *The Ancient Right of Sanctuary, Northumberland, Holy Island and the Farnes, Lewis Carroll in the North, Ghosts of Ripon, Ripon's Medieval Woodcarvers* and *Poverty and Health in Medieval Times*.

Mr Taylor has authored five books, edited several more and appeared on radio and TV.

He currently arranges and presents the Harrogate *Rossett* and Ripon *Wakeman* Lecture series for North Yorkshire County Council. He has also run adult education courses on *The History of Ripon, Ripon Cathedral* and *Lewis Carroll in the North*.

Rev. Derek Ching, MA, Cert. Ed. was raised in the Cotswolds. He read Geography at St Catharine's, Cambridge and gained a Certificate of Education there. Following military service with the Royal Irish Fusiliers, he taught at a boys' Grammar School near Birmingham before lecturing at Coventry College of Education and Warwick University. In his mid-40s he trained for the Church of England ministry at Queen's College, Birmingham. He served as a curate in Coventry then become Vicar of a group of rural parishes near Stratford on Avon.
Since retiring in 1996 he has lived in Ripon and often leads services in local churches.

Both authors are involved in interpretation/guiding at Fountains Abbey/Studley Royal, Ripon Cathedral and St Mary Magdalen's, Ripon (The Leper Chapel).

Acknowledgements

The authors thank the following for contributing to the publishing of this book:-

Assistance and advice: *Robert Adams, Bill Forster, Richard Hall and the Cathedral Vergers*

Proofreading: *Richard Bennett, Brian Crosse, David Lee and Bridget Milnes*

Indexing: *David Lee*

Photographs: *Ian Stalker, or as otherwise attributed*

Appendix information and assembly of text and images for printing: *Ian Stalker*

Other illustrations, artwork: *as indicated against each item*

Access to the Cathedral and records: *the Chapter of Ripon Cathedral*

Financing of printing: *The Friends of Ripon Cathedral*

Permission to quote: *Thomas Grœssinger and the executors of the late Dr Christa Grössinger, Dr Charles Tracy and the Lancashire and Cheshire Antiquarian Society.*

The authors particularly wish to acknowledge the help of Dr Charles Tracy and of the late Dr Christa Grössinger who carefully read through the text at various stages and made many valuable comments. However, the authors also wish to state that any errors or inconsistencies remain their responsibility.

Introduction

This is not the first book to describe the celebrated and rare medieval carvings done for Ripon Cathedral in the 15th century. Well-known scholars and enthusiasts have documented them before, notably the late Dr Christa Grössinger and Dr Charles Tracy. In addition, almost all of the books describing the building or architecture of the Cathedral include a section on the woodcarvings, especially the famous misericords, and many books about English cathedrals in general refer to Ripon's carvings.

As far as we know, this is the first book to concentrate on these carvings in particular: their origins, inspiration, creators and provenance. We also try to summarise the sometimes conflicting views of some specialists in church architecture as to the identity of the early carvers, what influenced them and how far afield their own labours or styles may have travelled.

The first mention of choir stalls is in 1088 at Maastricht. At about the same time there is a reference to misericordia in the regulations of a monastery at Hirsau in Germany, although it is not known if the seats had carvings under them. The earliest survivals in England are thirteenth century fragments in Hemingbrough, Kidlington, Durham Cathedral and Westminster Abbey and complete sets in Exeter and Salisbury[1].

We regard this book as an interim statement which, we hope, will stimulate further thought and research. We hope it will prove an easy and informative read, of interest to first-time visitors to the Cathedral as well as members of the congregation, volunteers and those with a wider interest in the subject.

All of the medieval woodcarvings are to be found in the western part of the Cathedral choir, in the area occupied by seating for designated churchmen and, more recently, women. To identify the position of particular items and their names, we start the book with a brief history of the choir and include diagrams describing this part of the Cathedral. These diagrams should also make useful references as the reader progresses through the book.

Publication has been sponsored by The Friends of Ripon Cathedral, for which the authors express their appreciation.

All numbered references in the text are documented at the end of the book, before the index.

The Choir

The long axis of the collegiate church at Ripon was divided by the choir screen, or pulpitum. To the west was the nave, the people's part of the building and to the east the choir, the part used by the clergy for daily worship.

In 1439, before the present choir stalls were built, the college of the church at Ripon is said to have comprised 32 members with duties in the choir, although it has been possible to identify only 31, comprising 7 canons, 6 vicars, 6 deacons, 6 thurifers (incense carriers) and 6 choristers. Today there are 34 seats – the extra two allocated, most likely, to the Wakeman (since 1604, the Mayor) and the Archbishop of York (now known as the cathedra, or bishop's seat).

Above: nave side of the pulpitum separating the nave from the choir

Below: choir side of the pulpitum with choir stalls (there is a larger picture on the outer back cover)

Apart from the crypt, which dates from Anglo-Saxon times, the building seen in Ripon today was never monastic – it was a church, served by canons (senior priests), each allocated a stall in the choir. They drew personal income from nearby estates called prebends, so they were also sometimes referred to as prebendaries, and were obligated to come together to

sing the daily services, although the vicars choral would usually deputise for them.

Over centuries the allocation of the choir-stalls changed, particularly after the Reformation. Behind some of the seats are written the names of saints. Obviously, the saints never occupied these particular seats – the inscriptions are merely in their honour.

In the mid-nineteenth century, the father of Lewis Carroll, Charles Dodgson, was installed as a residentiary canon at Ripon and had to reside for thirteen weeks each year, taking responsibility for reading the daily services and occupying the stall (seat) allocated to the Canon Residentiary. He was also appointed Archdeacon of Richmond, in which role he was entitled to a different stall in the Cathedral. Whether he sat in the seat now labelled Archidiaconatus de Richmond is unclear. A twentieth century list shows the Archdeacon of Richmond seated on the opposite side of the choir from the position now allocated.

Overleaf are two diagrams. The first explains names often given to parts of the choir woodwork. The second describes the numbering system used in this book to describe the stalls to the south (S) and north (N) sides of the pulpitum archway which leads from the nave to the choir. This diagram also shows the subjects carved on each misericord. The allocations shown are as they were understood to be in 1970.

Diagram 1

The Choir Stalls - Naming the Parts

Lateral stalls

Return stalls

Canopy

Stall uprights

Back stalls

Substalls

Stall upright

Seat Capping

Stall shoulder or arm rest

Misericord

Elbow

Tendril (branched)

Misericord Supporter

Standard, division or counter

Stall end

South Return Stalls

A/deacon of Richmond S4	Canon 3 S3	Canon 1 S2	Dean S1
Griffin with human leg	Lion, winged animal in fight	Angel, dated shield	C19th Angel

North Return Stalls

Canon in Residence N1	Canon 2 N2	A/deacon of Leeds N3	HC2 N4
Lion with upturned head	Wyvern and dogs	Angel, blank shield	Wyvern and birds

West Entrance under organ

Diagram 2

Naming and numbering of choir stalls

HC = Honorary Canon

N1, **S1**, etc. = misericord number used throughout this book

South Lateral

HC1 S5	Owl
HC3 S6	Mermaid
HC5 S7	Pig playing bagpipes
HC7 S8	Jonah cast overboard
HC9 S9	Man pushing woman in cart
Minor Canon S10	Fox and goose
Succentor S11	Griffin
HC11 S12	Antelope gorged and chained
HC13 S13	Pelican in her piety
HC15 S14	Jonah cast ashore
HC17 B. of Knaresb'gh S15	Samson and gates of Gaza
HC19 S16	C19th head
Bishop S17	Spies of Eschol

North Lateral

Foliage (fern)	HC4 N5
Flowers and foliage	HC6 N6
Lion and monkey	HC8 N7
Vine with grapes	HC10 N8
Two birds eating fruit	HC12 N9
Two antelope resting	Precentor N10
Fox preaching	HC14 N11
Fox and two geese	HC16 N12
Fox and two dogs	HC18 N13
Two dragons	HC20 N14
Green man	HCs 21,23 N15
Wild man	HCs 22, 24 N16
Griffin holding rabbit	Mayor N17

East end of choir stalls

The Carvers

The late fifteenth and early sixteenth centuries were the times when many of the major churches in the north were improving their choirs and fitting new stalls. New fittings that seem to have a close relationship appeared at Ripon around 1490, Manchester by 1506 and Beverley from 1520. Reconstruction was essential at Ripon following the collapse of two sides of the tower in 1458, which destroyed much of the choir. New stalls were carved between c.1489 and 1494. Fragments of earlier woodwork, with some of the earlier, less sophisticated carving, were incorporated into the aisle screens at this time. These screens are worth examining for their green men, cat masks and heads with protruding tongues. A piece of wood with the date 1379 was recorded in the north aisle before Sir George Gilbert Scott's restoration of 1864-68. The choir was formally re-opened on the 27th of January, 1868, in the presence of Bishop Bickersteth.

Collapse of the central tower in 1458 [Sketch from Canon J. Ashworth's *A Prospect of Ripon,* Ripon Cathedral 1975]

Who were the Ripon woodcarvers?

It is rare for the names of medieval craftsmen to have survived and Ripon is fortunate in being able to identify carvers' names. Three *hands* have been identified, referred to as Hands A, B and C[2]. It has been suggested, because of the limited quantity and superior quality of Hand A's work at Ripon – the north return stalls and organ loft – that this carver may have died or left quite early in the project.

A *Paper Book* of 1520, belonging to the Cathedral, contains the names of carvers working for the then Minster. Particular reference is made to the Bromflet family (variously spelled Bromfleet, Bromflete, Brownfleet, Brownfleitt), who may have come from York. Their connections with Ripon Minster are first mentioned in 1453 when Richard was involved with work on the pulpitum.

In 1519, William Bromflet is known to have been working for Bridlington Priory before returning to a project at Ripon. Bench ends, reputedly from Bridlington Priory, can now be seen at Leake Church by the A19 near Northallerton.

In 1520/21 a William Bromflet, surnamed Carver, worked at Ripon and was paid six pence a day; Christopher Bromflet was also paid six pence a day and Ranulph Bromflet was paid four pence a day. We also have names of other carvers working at the same time, including Robert Dowyff and Radulf Turrett, who were both paid four pence a day.

Historians have generally believed that William Bromflet was the lead carver. He was Wakeman (chief citizen) of Ripon in 1511 and is named in contracts as travelling to York and Hull arranging supplies.

Misericord N1: work attributed to 'Hand A', and compared to that of the Manchester master: *outstanding by any standards* (Tracy)

In recent years, his involvement in 1490 has been questioned. Charles Tracy suggests that he was 25-30 years old in 1506, and would have been too young to have carved the Ripon stalls in 1490. Tracy thinks that there is no evidence of Bromflet's 'hand' on the choir stalls themselves[3]. However, if he was the son of Richard Bromflete, known to have worked on the pulpitum in 1458 after the fall of the tower, he would be about 30 in 1489 and only in his early 50s as Wakeman in 1511. But would that make him too old - around 60 - to be working at Bridlington?

Misericord S12: work of 'Hand B'?

The Bromflet family had other associations with Ripon. In 1472/3, Richard Bromflete occupied land at Bishop Monkton with Robert Brownflete, chaplain and prebendary of Monkton. In 1478, there is a reference to John Carver, alias Brownfleitt, who was vicar from 1515 to after 1537. John Bromflet was successively procurator, chantry priest

Misericord N9: 'Hand C'?

and prebendary between 1531 and 1553. A man named Ranuld Bromflet died at Ripon in 1557 and a William Bromflet, carver, was admitted a freeman at York in 1482/3[4]. Dr Forster suggests that he may have been apprenticed to the Drawswerd family of carvers at York[5], where a Bromflet family is recorded from 1337 to 1483. The Victoria County History records that on 19th September 1383 Canon Thomas Bromflete exchanged/ transferred from the post of Canon of the chapel of the Blessed Virgin Mary and All Angels, York, to custos (mastership) of the chapel of St Mary Magdalen, Ripon. The last Bromflet listed as a freeman, after over a century of the family's recorded presence in the York area, was the William, Freeman of York, mentioned above.

Possible links with Beverley and Manchester Cathedrals

Sometimes, by comparing styles, it is possible to link carvings or carvers at different churches, but this can lead to difficulties. The stylistic links identified in the early twentieth century between the carvings at Ripon, Manchester and Beverley[7] have been re-assessed, notably in studies by Charles Tracy and Christa Grössinger. According to Tracy: *in spite of a general similarity in the seating at Ripon and Manchester there is no very close relationship*[8]. Sources other than Ripon are now considered to have had a more direct influence on the Manchester carvings, although Tracy suggests William Bromflet may have been loaned to Manchester, as he was later to Bridlington.

Table summarising Charles Tracy's assessment of
the work of three Ripon master carvers[6]

Carver	Probably worked on	Features of work
Hand A	• Seating and canopies of North Return stalls • Had probably left before Hand C arrived, the stylistic disjunction in NW corner evidencing a lack of collaboration between them	• Especially skilled at undercutting; noteworthy foliage with curling-up leaves, often placing an animal upon a leaf - imaginative work • Trademarks - the cut shoot running off the stem of supporters • Probably made the pulpitum loft and the crowned triple head
Hand B	• Entire south side - worked in C15th tradition • Provides the continuity between Hands A & C - his misericord dated 1489	• Crisp and skilful conventional work although lacks imagination • Uses traditional hawthorn and voluted trefoil leaves, as well as the more advanced pomegranate type • May have worked on the four major bench-ends • Trademarks - sprouting flower and crimped leaf
Hand C	• North lateral stalls • Major bench ends completed by Hands B and C by 1492	• Foliage carving is plastic, flat and uniform with little botanical accuracy • Most of his misericords have the same moulding profile; supporter stems recognised by distinctive bevelling and treatment of side shoots • Preference for incising over carving distinguishes his handling of pomegranate type from Hand B as stylised flower • He must have worked on bench ends and probably invented the characteristic hanging blossom • Specialised in leaves falling forward (also used by Hand B) • He probably carved the mayor's bench end, whose poppyhead incorporates the device dubbed by Purvis as the Aysgarth flower

Subjects Chosen for the Carvings

Compared with many medieval churches, Ripon has a large proportion of spiritual, moralistic and otherwise doctrinal carvings. No sponsor has been identified, so the canons probably commissioned the work themselves, as part of the restoration following the fall of the tower. Often, for misericords, profanity was the rule rather than the exception, giving a warning of the pitfalls of sin. Despite purges by the Puritans and Victorians, various scatological carvings survive elsewhere. Ripon's only example - a man exposing himself - is shown on page 56.

Did the carvers have a free hand?

Who decided what should be carved? There is no one answer to this question. Much probably depended on who was paying. Some sets include coats of arms associated with a benefactor. How much this was a gesture on the part of the carvers or the canons and how much it was a condition of the gift often is not clear. It is unlikely that the carvers got their ideas completely from where they liked, and later there is clear evidence for the use of patterns and pictures from books of hours, etc.

So where did the carvers' ideas come from? We can only touch on this here and the reader is referred to Dr Grössinger's *The World Upside Down,* chapter 2, for more information. The images in wood, paint, stone and metal that we find in medieval churches symbolise the beliefs and attitudes held at the time they were made. After printing was invented it became easier to identify sources. Early studies claimed that the first use of continental woodcuts, using printed books as the pattern, was at Ripon.

The Church's standpoint

In AD787 the Second Council of Nicea ruled *that the composition of religious imagery is not left to the initiative of artists but is formed upon principles laid down by the Catholic Church, and by religious tradition* and that *the execution alone belongs to the artist, the selection and arrangement of subjects belongs to the Fathers*[9] . However there is evidence in continental contracts that, although guidance was given, discretion was allowed to the carvers[10] .

The Forces of Evil

'Modern' representations of the dragons of Evil can be found on the 1920s War Memorial reredos behind the High Altar. Here the soldier saints – George and the Archangel Michael – are spearing four-legged, winged monsters.

Evil is often represented by a dragon of some kind, but it is not always obvious why particular kinds of dragon are used in particular contexts.

Some types of dragon found in mythology

Type	Description
Griffin (Gryphon)	Front eagle, rear lion. Four-legged with claws
Wyvern	Two legged – beast's head, bat's wings, eagle's legs and claws, serpent's tail
Basilisk (also known as Cockatrice)	Body and head of a cockerel, bat's wings, serpent's tail
Amphisbena	Four legs, with wings, two heads (one in tail)

In some places, other creatures are used, e.g.:
- the cunning fox deceives the gullible poultry (misericord N.11).
- the dogs attack the Lion of Judah (one explanation of N.1), but the dogs are good where they are the hounds of the Church catching the over-greedy fox (N.13). In the medieval world dogs licking the sores of a leper would be seen as bringing relief and comfort. (cf. dogs licking Lazarus' sores, Luke ch.16 v.21).

Note: pictures of all Ripon's misericord carvings can be seen towards the end of this book in the chapter *Notes on Individual Misericords*. The numbering system *N.1, S.1, etc.* is described in *The Choir* chapter at the start of the book.

Bestiaries

At Ripon, several mythological characters are derived from the *bestiaries*. A bestiary is a book, or poem, describing various animals and their habits, with stories about them, usually with a Christian interpretation or a moral. Although much in a bestiary is legendary, it was often taken to be factual, was translated into the vernacular and thus added to the body of popular belief.

Books in general

The development of printing in the fifteenth century brought a rapid dissemination of books such as the *Biblia Pauperum* from the Netherlands, illustrated with woodcuts. Although called the *Poor Man's Bible*, it must be remembered that it was read by the clergy, and not by ordinary people, although the pictures may have been used for teaching and to show the carvers what a patron had in mind.

The Romance of Reynard the Fox was particularly popular and its stories are represented in many carvings, not only at Ripon but across the country. A comparison of some of the illustrations with their related misericord at Ripon will illustrate the point (this and the facing page). Many of these were originally identified by Canon Purvis in the 1920s.

An example of a likely pictorial source for the carving subject: a noticeably similar image of Samson carrying off the gates of Gaza (misericord S.15)

Misericord S.9: the black and white photograph below left is thought to have been taken in the 1960s, since when the twig the woman is holding has been broken off. Carvings of the same scene can be found at Wrocław in Poland, and Baden-Baden, Germany. This was copied from the engraving by Master bxg and must have been one of the first such uses of continental prints in England[11].

As patterns for late fifteenth and early sixteenth century artists, Master P W of Cologne engraved suites of round playing cards. The one below is from his columbines set. Compare it with the columbines on the *Jonah cast overboard* misericord at Ripon (S.8). Other examples can be seen at Manchester and Beverley.

[Sketch on left from Grössinger, Christa *The World Upside Down*, Harvey Miller, 1997, p.65]

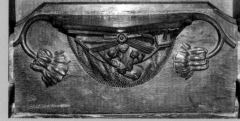

Other Ripon misericord details and early book
illustrations that may have influenced the carvers

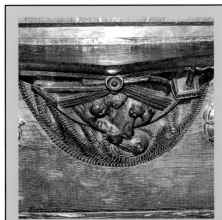  

Jonah cast overboard

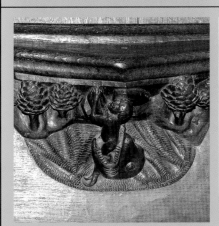  

Jonah returned by the whale

Caleb and Joshua
- the spies of Eschol

The Canopies

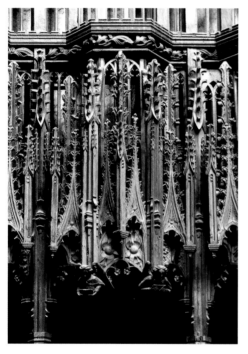

Ripon's Gothic canopy-work influenced much of the work that followed in the north of England. It was a strikingly different design concept when created, and regarded as the most intricate then attempted, With its many pinnacles and excrescences, it came to be called *spring top*.

But a design revolution twenty years later, at Manchester, saw a move away from the Gothic spring top style and the introduction of the *flat topped* Renaissance-style canopy. With joined rather than solid carved vaults in the lower zone, this marked a major shift in design between the two sets of canopies[12]. Practically, too, the canopies helped to reduce downdraughts.

Left: a section of Ripon's Gothic medieval canopies is shown (north stalls). The stalls' complex and intricate carving led to their description as *spring-top* (there is a larger picture on the inside back cover)

This engraving was dedicated to Charles Thomas Longley, Lord Bishop of Ripon, in about 1850. On the right, the double-width Bishop's Stall can be seen under its Gothic canopy. The other canopies are all of the flat-topped Renaissance style. Longley later became Bishop of Durham, Archbishop of York and then of Canterbury.

[Drawing by J. Bishop, lithograph by R. Groom, Ripon Cathedral collection]

In 1660, the spire on the central tower of Ripon Minster fell through the roof, destroying the canopies on the south side of the choir. After this, eight pointed Gothic canopies are reported to have been moved from the eastern end of the north range to the western end of the south range and replaced with flat-topped Renaissance (Jacobean) ones[13]. In the 1860s this later work was removed, to be replaced by Scott with reproductions in the fifteenth-century style, so that the eight easternmost canopies on the north and south sides are nineteenth century work.

This early 19th century drawing of the Ripon choir shows the Bishop's canopy and the combination of Gothic canopies (far left and right) and flat-topped Renaissance (Jacobean) canopies which were installed after the spire collapse of 1660.

[Lithograph from a drawing by Büchler, Ripon Cathedral collection]

The Pulpitum Loft

Tracy stated that *the polygonal pulpitum loft is unquestionably of the same build as the stall superstructure........The top levels of the wing screens at the west end have been left undecorated, suggesting that the organ loft was planned from the beginning*[14].

Above: the pulpitum loft.

Inset: this hand, to allow the organist to beat time for the choir, is late 17th century work, said to have been placed there before the organ had foot pedals. The hand can still be worked from the organist's new playing position.

Stalls and Bench Ends

At the west entry to the choir stalls, a symbol of evil on the Canon-in-Residence's stall opposes a symbol of Christ's power and goodness - the lion on the Dean's stall.

Opposing forces

A cockatrice on the Canon-in-Residence's bench end; a symbol of evil. Note the tip is missing from the tail

In contrast, the lion on the Dean's bench end denotes the beneficent powers of Christ

Two 1897 photographs from the Ripon Cathedral collection.

The one on the left shows the elephant and centaur on the Bishop's stall, the other the monkey on the Mayor's stall (right)

The Canon-in-Residence's Stall
Why a Cockatrice?

At Ripon the creature on the canon-in-residence's bench end is often referred to as a wyvern, representing the devil. Wyverns are usually shown with two legs, a serpent's tail and an animal's head, but this one has a beak and the hint of a cockscomb, suggesting a cockatrice or basilisk. The basilisk, or cockatrice, was the fabulous king of serpents, said to be hatched by a serpent from a cock's egg. It was reputed to be capable of *looking anyone dead on whom it fixed its eyes*[15]. Compare the picture on the right with the one on the previous page for damage to the end of the serpent's tail. The two pictures were taken about 10 years apart.

Recent damage is also obvious to the misericords S.9 (the branch held by the woman in the cart) and S.5 (the owl's talon).

Compare the wyvern shown on N.2 and N.4 on pp.44 and 46.

This older photo [M.H. Taylor] shows the undamaged tail on the cockatrice

The Bishop's Stall

The bench end of the Bishop's stall has a delightful collection of animals; real and mythological, and includes several human figures.

The Elephant

On top is the Ripon elephant, with a castle-like howdah on its back. It is extremely well carved, but mixes features of the two elephant sub-species. The domed forehead suggest it is an Indian elephant but its large ears call to mind its African cousin. Elephants from sub-Saharan Africa are not domesticated. The howdah contains eleven men and another man is held in the trunk. Sometimes, this is seen as a war elephant, the men being soldiers on their way to fight evil making it an appropriate symbol for a bishop or, we have assumed, the archbishop when the stalls were carved. The eleven can also be seen as the disciples of Jesus, with Judas held in the trunk. One of the eleven in the rear of the howdah is clearly modelled on the Ripon hornblower.

A lone elephant symbolised strength and wisdom, looking after the weak and dying members of its herd, but it could also represent carnal naivety because elephants mate for life and enjoy strong, deep relationships. People also believed the elephant was a mild, gentle creature, possessing the virtue of modesty.

Despite the apparent mixing of the two varieties, this carving is a good representation of an elephant. Others carved around the same time still repeat some of the oddities of Bestiary illustrations and other fanciful features. The best depictions of elephants on misericords are

those at Ripon and Beverley. The elephant was a favourite subject of medieval carvers and is nearly always shown with a castle on its back. Could it be another Scott 1860's replacement? If so, would Scott's carver have made the mistake about the ears? Or, could it be a re-carving after the damage of the 1660 spire collapse? It is noteworthy that the hornblower's hat is not the tricorn, which became the standard headgear during the eighteenth century. This would appear to support a seventeenth century or earlier origin for the carving, as a nineteenth century carver would surely have shown a three-cornered hat.

Louis IX of France gave an elephant to King Henry III in 1255. Crowds flocked to see it and Matthew Paris made a sketch (MS.16. F.ivr – Corpus Christi College, Cambridge).

Hornblower with 17th century hat

An elephant is carved on a thirteenth century misericord at Exeter and an elephant and howdah are mentioned in a deed of daring in the first book of Maccabees ch. 6. The Jews battled against King Antiochus, who had many elephants.

What is to be made of the creature on which the elephant stands – a turtle? There is a Hindu myth of the turtle swimming through the waters supporting an elephant which carries the people of the world safely through the depths, another image appropriate to the role of a bishop.

The Centaur

Half horse, half human, the centaur is well known in classical mythology as a wild and lawless

creature. It may seem surprising that a centaur should be found at the front of the bishop's stall. Though the mythical beasts could behave in a rather wild manner, they are often shown, armed with bow and arrows, opposing monsters on misericords, fonts, etc. This version may represent Chiron, the wise tutor and mentor to Jason and Achilles.

Perhaps the archbishop of the day saw his roles, as teacher of his people and opposer of the 'monsters' of heretical ideas, as appropriately shown in this way. Unfortunately, its design and position near an entry to the choir has meant it is very vulnerable to accidental damage.

The Bishop's Canopy

There is another uncertainty about the original Bishop's stall. This concerns its width. Hallett tells us: *The Jacobean canopy, which succeeded that of the fifteenth century, comprised the space of two stalls, as did also the modern structure by which it was itself succeeded and which is now in the Consistory Court.*

This suggests the following history since the late fifteenth century:

1480's - 1490's	Original canopy – two distinct stalls or one?
early 17th century	Jacobean canopy replaced original – double stall.
post 1660	New canopy constructed after severe damage by the fall of the spire – double stall.
1860's	New (present) canopy – two distinct stalls (part of Scott's restoration).

Likely stages in the design of the Bishop's stall

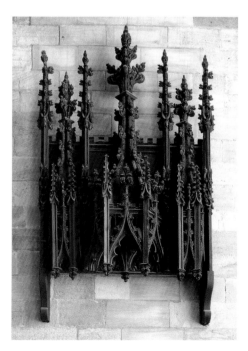

The post-1660 canopy, shown on the left, is presumed to be the one now suspended on the wall at the west end of the north nave aisle (the Chapel of Justice and Peace).

The Bishop's double canopy

24

The Mayor's stall

The Monkey

The monkey was regarded as a nasty evil creature embodying the vices of greed and deceit. Or is it meant to be an ape? The carving has much in common with the misericord N.7.

Apes were seen as highly sexed animals, chained to their passions, unable to break free. They are often depicted with the fox, the thief/trickster, deceiving the gullible.

An amusing tale accounts for the animal's presence on the Mayor's stall. The Wakeman (later Mayor) of Ripon was responsible for providing constables for the houses in the town. The fee was two pence for every door which faced the street. William Carver took advantage of this service, but blocked up his front door and built a back entrance to his house. Consequently, he refused to pay the fee. The argument with the Wakeman that followed prompted Carver to place the animal on the Wakeman's seat, making sure that the people, who were much more aware of symbols in the Middle Ages, associated the Wakeman with greed and deceit. The cleric organising the rebuilding seems to have been happy to allow this. A form of rough justice was exacted in 1511 when Carver became Wakeman of Ripon and had to sit in the same seat!

A bracket for the mace was fixed in 1646[16].

The monkey - a carver's revenge
on the Wakeman of the day?

Seats and Misericords

What is a misericord?

Misericords are the ledges, or brackets, attached to the tip-up seats of the choir stalls, usually in the choir of a cathedral, collegiate or minster church, which allowed the worshipper to take the weight off his legs but still, technically, to stand for prayer. They are often referred to as 'mercy' or 'pity' seats.

It is important to remember that the seats were 'up' most of the time so that the existence of carving here is perfectly logical. The only times that the Canons were allowed to use the seats during the Offices were at the Epistle and the Gradual at Mass, and the Responses at Vespers.

There are two other historical uses of the word *misericord*:

>(i) a room of a monastery, often the infirmary, where some relaxation of the monastic rule was permitted and meat could be eaten;

>(ii) a small dagger used to deliver a death stroke to a fatally wounded enemy and thus take pity on him.

In most cases, the misericord seat was set at about 30cm high and was around 64cm wide. Most were made from a solid piece of oak. The underside of the ledge was decorated with a carving, occasionally religious but more often not. Later the knobs on the armrests, known as elbows, and the bench ends were also often decorated with carvings.

English misericords developed differently from continental ones by having 'supporters' added – an extra decoration on either side of the central carving, which gave scope to comment on or extend the main theme. Occasionally supporters and main carving offer a linked narrative, at other times they are merely decorative space-fillers. Examples of both can be found at Ripon.

Maurice H. Taylor

Leaf pattern tie – Beverley

It is worth noting the shapes of misericord seats in different parts of the country to help to identify particular sets, regional styles and dates of construction. The bracket edges can be straight, concave, or convex. Manchester's, for example, have similarities to the Ripon seats but without Ripon's 'bulge'. Beverley is the only set that has embattled or scalloped detail around the seat edge. Students of misericords note if the supporters have been shaped into circles, squares or diamonds and how the tendrils of the supporters curve around the central scene, have branches or shoots, or leaf ties as at

Manchester, Beverley and Windsor. The angle of the seat elbows is also important – at Ripon the elbows of the north return stalls are horizontal, but the north lateral ones are at 30° to the horizontal.

Positioning of the Misericords

There seems to be no record of the detailed processes by which a particular misericord ended up in its present position; indeed, it is quite possible that some are not in their original positions.

Surely the official occupants of the Ripon stalls at that time would, at least, be consulted about the nature of their misericord and possibly have commissioned it. As an example, the intriguing case of the Scimitar Oryx (S.12) is discussed on pages 38–9.

Some of the prebendaries and other clerics who approved/commissioned the carvings would be happy to sit upon/hold down/squash the forces of Evil. Others wished to have significant Old Testament scenes and there are proportionally more of these than in sets elsewhere – four out of thirty-four.

Ripon's Old Testament scenes were all regarded as important in the Middle Ages because they were a prefiguring of scenes in the Life of Christ. These are listed below.

Misericord number	Showing	Biblical reference	Prefiguring Christ's
S8	Jonah thrown out of the ship	Jonah ch.1 v.15	CRUCIFIXION
S14	Jonah cast ashore	Jonah ch.2 v.10	RESURRECTION
S17	The return of the Spies	Numbers ch.13 v.23	BAPTISM
S15	Samson taking the Gates of Gaza	Judges ch.16 v.3	BURSTING OUT OF HELL

The four carvings on Ripon's misericords that derive from the Bible

All four certain biblical examples are copied from illustrations in the *Poor Man's Bible*.

Dating Misericords

First recorded in the eleventh century, misericords are still occasionally being carved today. Many were destroyed during the Commonwealth period and yet more by the Victorians. In England, the earliest complete sets survive from the thirteenth century at Exeter and Salisbury[17]. Francis Bond[18] identified, *with more or less certainty*, 32 fourteenth century sets; 43 fifteenth century sets; 15 sixteenth century sets and 7 seventeenth century sets. Canterbury Cathedral commissioned a set from Sir George Gilbert Scott in 1879 and the Marquis of Ripon had a set incorporated into the 1870's church of St Mary at Studley Royal.

The construction of Ripon's present choir-stalls is usually dated to between 1489 and 1494, but they may have been started a little earlier. In the south return stalls is a demi-angel with shield bearing the date 1489.

The pictures displayed on the opposite page illustrate this. The form of the number '4' is similar to that on two carvings at Fountains Abbey. The one shown here has '1494' on a corbel high in the gable of the west end and there is another showing '1483' on an angel in the Chapel of the Nine Altars. It appears in similar form at Winchester St Cross Hospital.

In 1958 Ripon Cathedral accepted a bequest of a misericord, thought to be thirteenth century and said to be one of the set removed from the stalls when the fifteenth century set was carved and installed.

Two men in armour, their visors lifted, face each other in combat. In the centre background a tall tree spreads its branches about them. This could represent the Conflict between good and evil or is possibly part of a story sequence.

Dr Grössinger cautions that it may be a fake (personal correspondence).

[Adapted from an original photograph by M.H. Taylor]

The shield on this Ripon misericord (S.2) is dated 1489 but the misericord could have been carved during the 1490s and pre-dated[19].

Below left: the Bishop's bench end bears the date 1494 to indicate the completion of the choirstalls, but close inspection of the bench end suggests it is partly nineteenth century work.

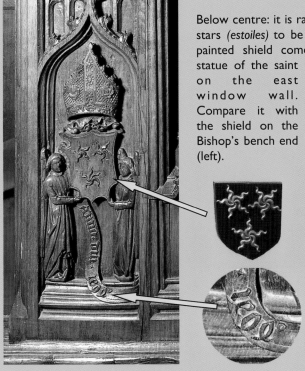

Below centre: it is rare, possibly unique to Ripon, for wavy stars (estoiles) to be used as a symbol of St Wilfrid. The painted shield comes from the 1920s Ninian Comper statue of the saint on the east window wall. Compare it with the shield on the Bishop's bench end (left).

Above: a Fountains Abbey angel dated 1483. Note the old form of the digit '4', common to all three carvings on this page.

Notes on Individual Misericords

In this review we give what appears to be the most plausible current explanation of what the misericords show and, where possible, a symbolic meaning even if occasionally this latter is somewhat tentative. In some cases we also give an alternative view; especially if another explanation has been popular, or seems to be an interesting variant. We look at the supporters and elbows in some instances, especially where they are an integral part of the story or are of intrinsic interest.

Rickman 20

Abbreviations used in the following pages:
(looking at the underside of the seat from the front)
S = misericord on **South side of choir**
N = misericord on **North side of choir**
1, 2, etc. = **numerical position, starting from the west choir access archway, below the organ**
R.S. = **Right supporter**
L.S. = **Left supporter**
R.E. = **Right elbow**
L.E. = **Left elbow**

White Rose in
Soleil
(See Note 2 below)

Notes on the illustrations and text in this section

1. Many of the ancillary features show a stylised leaf, flower or fruit form, sometimes so stylised as to be difficult to identify positively – even if they were intended to be specific varieties when carved.

2. We have called the five-petalled rose a 'Tudor' rose, but it should be remembered that the roses of both York (pictured above) and Lancaster also have five-petals, which can be double or even triple.

3. We have tried to show the actual shape of the underside of each choir stall seat. Each photograph has been adjusted to an approximately true rectangular shape and the relationship between the width and depth of seat in the photo is similar to that of the original. The measurements used to accomplish this are shown in the Appendix (page 64).

4. Misericords will be described in numerical order, starting with the South Side stalls. Diagram 2 on page 9 may prove a useful reference when reading this section.

SOUTH SIDE STALLS

S.1 (The Dean's Stall) – A demi-angel (half angel) holding a book or a shield
(Restored during Scott's refurbishment in the 1860s)

Is the angel holding a book or a shield? Opinion is divided. The size and the way it is held suggests book, but the shape suggests a shield. If a shield, it could bear St George's cross; if a book, it is possibly either a symbol of learning or the Book of Life, where the deeds of everyone are recorded for Judgement Day.

    Supporters – both double-petalled roses.
    R.E. – a rose – but possibly also an 1860s restoration – different in style to others nearby.
    L.E. – a pomegranate (damaged).

S.2 A demi-angel holding a shield (or plaque) with the date '1489'

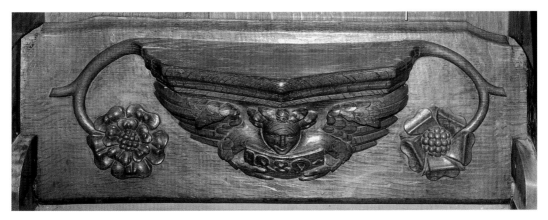

See page 29 regarding the style of the number '4'.

The angel's costume appears to be made of feathers. In the medieval mystery plays it was common practice for angels to wear a costume of feathers.

R.S. – a single rose in a pentangle form.

L.S. – a tudor rose.

R.E.– a pomegranate (split) – side view. The fruit is often shown like this to emphasise "the many held in unity".

S.3 A Lion and a Dragon fighting

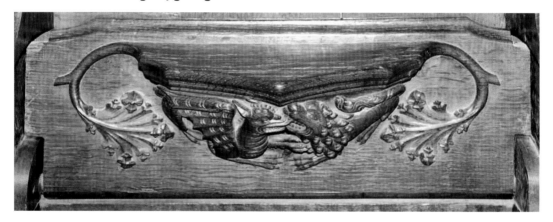

Good fighting Evil. The Dragon symbolises the Devil. The Lion is usually a symbol of Good, except when he is attacking a human although the Bestiary tells us that the lion is merciful to a prostrate man. (see also N.1)

Supporters – stylised vine leaves – the one on the left is rather better carved.

S.4 Griffin (Gryphon) devouring a human leg

This winged, four-footed creature (part lion, part eagle) tears its human victims to pieces and devours them in its nest/lair.

    Supporters – stylised vine leaves (similar to S.3 but not as elaborately cut).

S.5 An owl facing front with staring eyes and outstretched wings

Most species of owl are nocturnal i.e. they do not fly or hunt in the day as it is too bright for them. The owl then, became associated with those who would not see the light of Christ's teaching – and especially the Jews.

Rather oddly, this carving seems to be most like a Little Owl which does fly in daylight in our part of the world. It is noteworthy that this owl is in the darkest corner of the stalls.

    Supporters – two double roses virtually identical, but six-petalled, so not the Tudor roses.

    R.E. – thistle heads – often associated symbolically with thorns and thus showing suffering, pain, sorrow. See Genesis ch.3 v.17, 18 (Adam's curse) and, by extension, Christ's Crown of Thorns.

S.6 A Mermaid holding a mirror and a brush.

The voluptuous sea-maiden lures men to their doom. The symbolism of the mirror is very complex but here seems to reinforce the vanity theme. In the old folk song *The Mermaid* she has a comb and a glass in her hand; here a brush, very delicately carved.

    R.S. – a double rose (side view). Copied from a German 'playing card' pattern.

    L.S. – a clover (side view) – three-leaved clover is one of the symbols of the Holy Trinity.

Quite how one interprets the supporters in relation to the main carving is somewhat problematic in this case. The same point would apply in many other cases in Ripon and elsewhere.

S.7 *Piglets dance to a one-drone bagpipe played by a sow*

The pig is often regarded as symbolizing lust and gluttony and the bagpipes as a low-status instrument used to rouse uncontrollable passions. Perhaps, the carver and/or the sponsor associated the skirl of the pipes with the squealing of pigs! Here both the piper and piglets

34

seem very intent on serious practice of both music and dance. Note that the instrument here has a double chanter with single drone. In other contexts angels are occasionally found playing bagpipes, which challenges the use of the instrument solely for the arousal of lustful passions.

Notes:

1. Fifteenth century pigs still had the stiff 'comb' down their backs which has been bred out in most modern breeds. Even though generally the animals the artists knew well were hardly ever realistically carved, those of the Ripon carvers include many naturalistic details.

2. In the late 15th century several areas of England were well-known for their piping, while in Scotland bagpipes were only gradually coming to the fore after James I of Scotland, an accomplished piper himself, encouraged the playing of the instrument.

    R.S. – a rose reversed (it appears to be six-petalled).

    L.S. – a Tudor rose.

S.8 *Jonah is thrown overboard*

The ship is medieval (note the stern castle). A superb copy of an illustration in the *Poor Man's Bible*[21]. This incident was regarded as important because it was a foretelling of our Lord's death – specifically here his entombment (see the Book of Jonah and Matthew ch.12 v.40).

> **S. (both)** – columbines. Because of its supposed resemblance to a dove (in Latin – *Columba*) the columbine is especially associated with the Holy Spirit, frequently portrayed as a dove. Others saw the same flower as more eagle-like, giving it its

alternative name aquilegia. One of the symbolic meanings of the eagle is Christ's Ascension, so, perhaps, the symbolism was looking forward to the triumph of that event after the sadness of our Lord's death.

S.9 *A bearded man wheels a woman in a three-wheeled barrow*

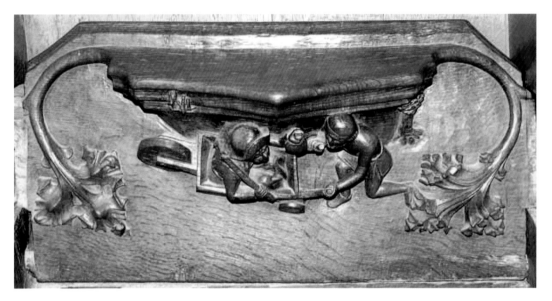

She holds a bottle in one hand and a twigged stick in the other. This is a copy of an engraving by a German artist Master 'bxg' (see page 16), which was used to illustrate the story of a peasant trying to get his somewhat inebriated wife to work or home.

Dr Grössinger tells us: *depictions ridiculing women were extremely popular around the turn of the fifteenth/sixteenth centuries, often showing them as viragos and gossips.* She adds: *The woman in the three-wheeled barrow – it has three wheels in the print by Master bxg and also in a French manuscript of c.1475 – where the woman holds a flail, and is being taken to the fields; it is thought that three wheels were easier along muddy paths. What is sure is that barrows were used to take muck and dung, and if human beings were carted in them it was for punishment and in disgrace. The dry stick that does not flower is a Carnival symbol, and barrows were used then too. In the print, the woman also has a goitre which was a sign of stupidity*[22].

Popular association links this misericord with the St. Cuthman legend – the Saxon saint who pushed his aged mother about in a wheelbarrow while he preached to the people of Sussex – eventually founding Steyning church. The basic elements of the Cuthman story – especially the wheelbarrow – are the same as the German story and it is a possibility that the carver and/or commissioning cleric had the Cuthman story in mind. This would be regarded as very appropriate as Cuthman may have been working in Sussex at the same time as St. Wilfrid. The Cuthman story is told in Christopher Fry's play *The Boy with the*

Cart.   Dr Grössinger asks: *Do you think [the woman in the cart] would have been a good example as mother of a saint?*

Lucius Smith[23] contends that the carving represents Pontius Pilate wheeling Judas Iscariot down into Hell. Though fascinating, no other researcher adopts this interpretation, which includes a reversal of roles with the imperial governor doing the hard work giving a ride to a member of a subject people.

S.10 *A fox stealing a goose*

(see also N.11, 12 and 13)

This reflects a very common medieval story of the craftiness of Reynard the Fox, here taking away a goose.

> **Supporters** – these are an integral part of the story: a woman with a distaff and a dog stand on stylised leaves and appear to be giving chase. This is a warning of the consequences for the gullible, trusting Christian (the goose) who can be easily caught by the cunning Devil (the fox).
>
> Chaucer's *Nun's Priest's Tale* is sometimes cited as a version of this story but in that narrative Reynard is up against Chanticleer the Cock, who proves to be as crafty as his captor and gets away.
>
> **Question**: was this misericord originally designed to go with the 'triple cartoon' on the North side – say, between misericords N.12 and N.13?

S.11 *A Griffin*

Half animal, half bird, this mythical creature is a combination of the King of the Beasts (the Lion), and the King of the Birds (the Eagle). A problem here is that the hind legs – the Lion part – have cloven hooves. Compare S.4 and N.17. Did the carver make a mistake?

The Griffin is very hostile to horses and also tears humans to pieces (see notes on S.4 – where the carver has given the hind legs claws).

S.12 *An antelope gorged and chained*
(See also N.10)

The scimitar or white oryx is closely akin to the ibex, which also has serrated horns, but straighter. In heraldry, this would be called a hart, one of several generic terms for different kinds of deer and antelope.

Almost invariably portrayed as male, the stag has antlers reminiscent of the tree of life and is a creature of beauty, grace and agility, often opposed to evil monsters (similar to the lion and the eagle). In the Middle Ages the way of solitude and purity – the hermit way of life – was symbolized by the stag which, in the desert fringes, spent much of the year alone among rocky outcrops. The two horns symbolize the Old Testament and the New Testament, the twin bases of Christian life.

The hart, in Psalm 42 v.1 – best known in the form of the hymn *As pants the hart for cooling streams* – can be seen as a straight-forward reference to the Christian soul thirsting for God. However, it may refer to the enmity between stags and dragons. One of the stories about this deadly opposition tells of the stag becoming thirsty because of the hot breath of the dragon; the stag then finds a cooling stream and fills his belly with water. He then squirts the water into the dragon's lair and, as the dragon emerges soaking and confused, kills it with his antlers.

It is possible that this is an unusual type of misericord – a political statement. Two scimitar oryx were the supporters of the arms of Henry VI. They were not used in this way by any other monarch although the badge of his father, Henry V features an oryx with a similar coronet and chain, which seems to have been copied here[24]. Henry VI was the last Lancastrian King (1422-1461); with a brief return (1470-71) before he was murdered. The gorge or collar is a coronet suggesting a royal theme, but the underlying motive is not clear. For other information about the scimitar oryx refer to N.10.

A record of 1502-3[25], at the time the south aisle was being completed, gives a list of images in the Minster, including several consecrated in the latter years of the 15th century. Remarkably, this includes an image of King Henry VI. Clearly, a generation after his murder in 1471, Henry VI was still revered by churchmen in Ripon, and seemingly throughout England, as a very devout monarch of almost saintly status.

This suggests that the sponsor of misericord S.12 was more likely to be an admirer of Henry VI than an opponent.

To maximise income from pilgrims, the Clergy encouraged not only as large a donation as could be afforded at the main St Wilfrid shrine but also offerings at the numerous saintly images near the pilgrim route around the Minster.

S.13 *The pelican in her piety*

A popular story in the Bestiary has the pelican killing her chicks because they annoy her and, after three days, she revives them by pecking her breast and allowing her blood to flow over them. This is a very powerful Resurrection symbol. The pelican is the equivalent of Christ shedding his blood for the salvation of Mankind, in other words, giving us new Life after Death. The bird carved here is not at all pelican-like, but when pelicans are at

rest on water, the tip of the bill touches the breastbone.

Supporters – two lions' faces with protruding tongues. In the Bestiary there is a very similar story to the pelican and chicks in which the lioness gives birth to her cubs who are dead for three days. The father lion then comes and breathes life into them, awakening them with his roar. This story – of the many related to Lions (see for example N.7) – may be the one alluded to here.

S.14 *Jonah comes out of the Whale*

(refer to S.8)

After three days in the belly of the Whale (Jonah ch.2 v.10) he is spewed out onto the shore. This is a powerful pre-figuring of the resurrection of Christ from the dead. The

40

Apostles' Creed states that: *Jesus was crucified, died and was buried; he descended to the dead. On the third day he rose again;* (the older version has: *he descended into hell*).

Jesus himself quotes the Jonah story as a foretelling of his own Crucifixion and Resurrection (e.g. Matthew ch.12 v.39-41). Clearly this is copied from the *Poor Man's Bible*.

> **R.S.** – a very curious creature – bat, mouse or even a beast of Hell[26]? No one seems certain.

S.15 *Samson carrying away the gates of Gaza*

The story of Samson's visit to Gaza is told in Judges ch.16 v.1-3. The Philistines discover that Samson is in the city and close the gates, intending to deal with him in the morning. But, in the middle of the night, Samson gets up, breaks the gates down and walks off with them.

In medieval times, this story was seen as another powerful pre-figuring of Jesus rising from the dead and bursting out of the tomb or, as many saw it, bursting the Gates of Hell to set the Devil's captives free. Again, this has been copied from the *Poor Man's Bible*. This misericord is unique in the British Isles and was chosen for display at the Victoria and Albert Museum as part of the major exhibition of 'Gothic' work in 2003.

S.16 *A man's head with flowing hair and beard*

This is a Victorian carving, done by one of Sir George Gilbert Scott's craftsmen during the 1860s restoration. For a long time before the Victorian restoration the archbishop – then after 1836, the bishop – had a double stall but, it seems, only one misericord seat. The records do not tell us when the archbishop was allotted this double stall (see the summary

on page 24). When Scott came to restore the choir stalls to their original, fully-canopied state, the bishop's seat was divided into two. Hence, a new misericord was needed. Note – the pre-1860 archbishop's canopy is preserved at the west end of the north nave aisle in the Chapel of Justice and Peace, which was consecrated in 2006. It is certainly big enough to cover two stalls.

S.17 (The Bishop's Stall) – the return of the spies

Moses sent out twelve spies (one from each tribe) to gather information about the lie of the land, the nature of the people and the products grown (see Numbers ch.13 and following, noting especially verses 23 and 24). Here is Joshua, who became leader after Moses' death, accompanied by Caleb of the tribe of Judah. They have picked such an enormous bunch of grapes that they need to carry it on a pole between them. This seems an odd way to carry a load suspended on a pole - or is it odd? Joshua leads, but they are out of step.

Symbolic Points in this image:

- this is an Old Testament story given a Christian slant
- the Bunch of Grapes is larger than real life. Wine is the blood of Christ in Christian worship and, by extension, the grapes become a symbol of the body of Christ. Jesus Christ is far and away the most important person who ever lived so, as His importance cannot be exaggerated, the bunch of grapes can be truly gigantic in size. On the comparable misericord at Beverley Minster, the bunch is even bigger in relation to the men
- Joshua, one of the great Jewish heroes, cannot see Christ whereas Caleb – a *future Christian* of the tribe from which Our Lord's earthly family came – has Christ in view all the time
- a late fifteenth century Christian sponsor would see the two figures out of step as emphasising the point above. Joshua, representing those continuing in the Jewish faith, is out of step with those who have seen the light and follow Christ (see S.5).

Supporters: these may represent some of the inhabitants of Canaan:

L.S. – a headless human – his head is in his torso. Described by the Latin author Pliny the Elder in his *Natural History* as a *blemya*, sometimes also called an *anthropophagus*.

R.S. – a head on legs (no body). Possibly represents the *anakin* the spies saw in Canaan.

These supporters are sometimes referred to as *Mr Somebody* and *Mr Nobody*.

A Jewish visitor remarked that Joshua and Caleb being out of step could possibly speak to Jews as symbols of the Davidic Kingdom and its division, after Solomon's death, into the Northern Kingdom of Israel - ten tribes, usually dominated by Ephraim - and the southern kingdom of Judah - two tribes, Judah and Benjamin. These two kingdoms were frequently *out of step*. This 'interfaith' interpretation was clearly not in the mind of the original carver or his sponsor.

NORTH SIDE STALLS

N.1 (Stall of the Canon-in-Residence) – a lion attacked by dogs

Two quite different interpretations have been suggested here:

    (a)   The lion symbolises Christ who is being attacked by dogs on the way to His crucifixion. While there is no evidence for this in the Gospels, it was a common traditional story and this picture is found on misericords and in other illustrations elsewhere.

    (b)   However it could be interpreted as the lion symbolising evil, as it sometimes does. See for example 1 Peter ch.5 v.8: *Our enemy the devil, like a roaring lion, prowls around looking for someone to devour.* The dogs then become the forces of good driving evil away (see also N.2 and N.13). But, are these dogs sheltering in the vine leaves in N.2? Dogs licking the sores of lepers etc. were thought to bring relief.

N.2 A wyvern

(see also N.4)

The wyvern is a two-legged, winged dragon, so will certainly represent evil. It has also been suggested that the creatures on the supporters are calves and not dogs. Do they have ears or horns? Young and inexperienced calves are often viewed as symbols of innocence. In this instance their sheltering in the vine leaves may represent the protection offered by Christ's Church (see N.7). Calf symbolism, however, can be more complex. The calf is associated with St Luke, whose Gospel was said to fill the air with sound Christian teaching, rather than noisy bellowing! The main carving here is clearly an insert but we cannot now be certain when and why this was necessary. It would appear to be by the same carver as N.4.

Above: N.2 A wyvern

N.3 A demi-angel holding a blank shield
(compare S.2)

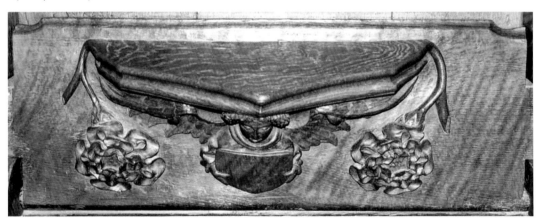

It has been suggested that the shield might have been painted with the occupant's coat of arms. There is an unresolved question as to whether misericords were sometimes painted – if so, was this up to individual carvers or – more likely – their sponsors?

N.4 A wyvern

A very similar carving to N.2. The two birds on the supporter leaves could be Christian souls safe from the evil Wyvern as long as they stayed in the Tree of Life. More specifically, this could be the *Peredexion* or *Perindens* tree in India with delicious fruit much sought after by birds (such as doves) which also nest in the tree. The dragon has to move frequently while waiting to catch a dove leaving the shelter of the tree (God the Father) as it cannot live in the tree's shadow (God the Son). The fruit is the Wisdom of the Holy

Spirit. The moral would then be that the tree (the Trinity) gives us all our needs, but, if we turn away from God, we will be devoured by evil (see also N.9).

N.5 *Hart's tongue fern*

During the nineteenth century, this beautifully flowing carving was identified as a hart's tongue fern *Scolopendrum vulgare*. The symbolic significance is not entirely clear but: *These ferns are said to represent the flourishing of spiritual knowledge* (Harrison). Perhaps the carver appreciated the flowing, frond-like leaves of this fern which is found in shady, damp places and regarded it as a particular challenge to reproduce the structure. Late medieval herbalists used a preparation from this plant in the treatment of a number of ailments – particularly liver complaints.

N.6 *A very elaborate flower*

In his classic work *Misericords* (1910), Bond wrote: *In this department of foliated ornament the Ripon carvers easily bear off the bell.... unequalled elsewhere, except perhaps in some pretty columbines at Manchester. In Beverley Minster are copies, more or less clumsy, of the Ripon design.*

> **Supporters** – these are an integral part of the design with two smaller, similar flowers. All three flowers are variations on a theme of floral exuberance but none has been positively identified. Both flowers could be early stages in the development of the mature flower.

N.7 *A lion attacking a monkey in a vine*

The medieval bestiaries tell us that *a sick lion will seek out an ape and devour it in order to be cured*[27]. Harrison has the lion representing good-living Christian folk triumphing over the ape – symbol of greed and deceit. The monkey attempts to escape from the lion by climbing a grape vine. In practical terms, this action appears to be fatally stupid, as even a sick lion could deal with any prey hiding in a grape vine!

The symbolism of the picture is all-important. The sinful monkey attempts to escape the 'wrath to come' by sheltering within bunches of grapes – one of the Christ symbols – (see S.17). Those who live evil lives return to the Church for salvation – even at the point of death.

A rather more jocular interpretation runs like this: the sick lion is a patient needing to be cured. The ape is often shown with attributes of a medieval doctor – frequently holding a urine bottle. This reflects the considerably lower esteem in which the medical profession was held in the middle ages. There appears to have been a standing medieval joke that if you go to the doctor, he'll give you all kinds of potions, etc. to make you well – but it would do you far more good to eat your doctor than swallow his medicines!

N.8 *A vine with four bunches of grapes*

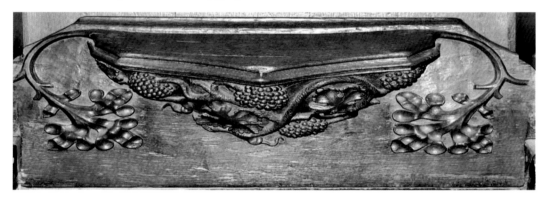

Christ is the True Vine and gave his blood for the salvation of mankind. The juice of the vine is an important element in the communion service or Mass (although, by the late fifteenth century, it was regarded as so precious in the western Church, that only the priest partook of the wine).

Why four bunches? The disciples were enjoined by Jesus to preach the Gospel in all the world. The 'four corners of the earth' was a way of speaking of the whole world and the four gospels form the cornerstones of the Christian message.

> **Supporters** – larger versions of the leaves in the main carving. This is one of three entirely vegetable carvings by the north side carver, the others being N.5 and N.6.

N.9 *Two birds in a bush pecking at fruit*

While it is not possible to identify the exact species, the two birds are probably passerines of the sparrow/finch family. The fruit looks very blackberry-like. Grössinger identifies it as symbolising *Christian souls eating of the fruits of salvation*[28]. Although an obvious danger is not present, this could be seen as a simplified version of the birds perched in the tree story in N.4.

Note that the elbows between N.9 and N.10 are demon heads, quite unlike anything else at Ripon (illustrated on p.58).

N.10 *Two antelope resting above a rabbit warren*

These antelope are called scimitar oryx because of the curved nature of their horns. They can be compared with the heraldic oryx in S.12 and are related to stories in the bestiaries. The serrations on the horns are very like saw-teeth in this picture. The two horns represent the Old and New Testaments (guides for the good Christian life) but an unwary oryx can get its horns caught in a thicket and can then be easily caught by a hunter (the Devil). The unwary Christian can be ensnared by drunkenness and other vices into the Devil's clutches. *Wine and Women will make men of understanding to fall away*, the Apocryphal book of Ecclesiasticus tells us (ch.19 v.2).

But all is not lost as the oryx can, given time, saw through the entrapping branches; or, perhaps, as may be the case here, a trapped oryx – is the right hand one caught? – can rely on another oryx to assist him to break free. (Christians help each other in the mutual struggle with the evil one). The significance of the association with the rabbit warren is not clear.   Are the oryx guarding the warren? (see N.17 for comments on rabbits). The political significance of the scimitar oryx is discussed under S.12.

N.11, N.12 and N.13: 'The fox misericords'

These three misericords are in a sequence, which show scenes from a version of the traditional story of Reynard the Fox .

N.11 *The cunning fox preaching to a goose and a cockerel*

(see notes on S.10 about Chanticleer the cock).

It is generally accepted that three of the four birds in N.11 and N.12 are geese, but this raises some unresolved questions:

- why is the N.11 goose more like the passerines in N.9 than the geese in N.12?
- is the goose in N.11 meant to be a duck, as some have suggested?
- are all three geese carved by the same carver?

N.12 *The fox with two geese*

The fox has beguiled his listeners but shows his true colours by catching two of his prey and taking them off for dinner. The cock has been replaced by a goose.

N.13 *The fox caught by the hounds* (pictured on next page)

In the set at Beverley Minster the fox ends up being hanged. At a simple level one can read this as a fable that, however crafty and cunning you may be, if you are too greedy you will not succeed. At a higher level, this can be seen as a comment on the activities of the clerics generally but particularly the friars, who had moved away from the early zealous missionary work and ascetic life of their early thirteenth century origins and had become, by the late fifteenth century, wealthy, comfortable and 'part of the establishment'. The fox (the greedy friar) had beguiled the congregation with his smooth tongue and had then tried to grab too much to add to his already plentiful store and is easily caught or exposed by the hounds of the Church, watchdogs of the local community – and, of course, beyond reproach themselves! See notes under S.10, which, perhaps, should be part of this sequence. One curious technical problem is that the profile of the misericord ledge (or corbel) of N.13 is different from all the others in the line. Possibly it has been rather crudely repaired.

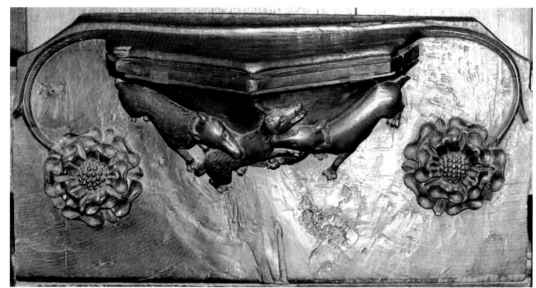

Above: N.13 *The fox caught by the hounds*

N.14 *Two dragons fighting*

Depending how you look at each case, something like ten of Ripon's thirty-four misericords illustrate a conflict or potential conflict situation. This is the only case where the fight is between two equals. Whatever form the Dragon takes it always represents Evil.

These are *amphisbenae* – dragons with two heads, one in the usual position, the other at the end of its tail. It is winged with two clawed legs. Perhaps it represents an encouragement to the struggling Christian that the forces of Evil do sometimes fall out among themselves.

N.B. The only surviving misericord thought to be from Ripon's early fourteenth century set is in the treasury (see p.28). It also shows two equals fighting but, in this case, two knights in armour on foot. This is possibly not the same symbolism as suggested above – it may have been part of a story sequence.

N.15 *A Green Man upside down*

The head has luxuriant foliage emerging from the mouth, a classic green man/cat mask feature – compare the stone carving inside the north-west tower (above the cathedral shop area). Sometimes this creature is referred to as Jack-in-the-Green.

The Green Man is a very common pagan symbol of fertility and plenty, often seen in grotesques and gargoyles outside churches, for example in the carving on the north-east corner of the chapel of the nine altars at Fountains Abbey. One problem with this is its non-human features, with wool instead of hair and sheep-like ears. Grössinger suggests it is a mask[29].

It is sometimes contended that such an obvious pagan symbol was not allowed inside a church but, clearly, there was no such hard and fast rule in Ripon. The tradition, that such symbols, grotesques and monsters were placed on the outside to alert the sinner to the need for redemption, is fallacious according to Friar. He points to the doom-filled wall paintings inside churches, evident from the Romanesque period on, and the carvings of pagan symbols in gargoyles, roof bosses, etc.[30].

In 601 Pope Gregory the Great advised against destroying pagan shrines; rather they should be purified with holy water, so that pagan sites, feasts and elements of pagan worship were steadily assimilated into Christian practice, with relics replacing idols. Over time this created the iconographical and cultural ambivalence we see today. The Green Man reputedly symbolises the *endurance of nature that was Christianised to represent the everlasting life promised by a belief in Jesus Christ*[31].

N.16 *A wild man carrying a club in an oak wood (the wodehouse)*

The wild man or wodehouse (various spellings) is a forest dweller who, in some versions of the popular medieval story, has been brought up by animals in the forest. Friar suggests that he is a symbol of strength and wholesomeness, is superior to all other creatures, and is therefore a worthy leader as King of the Forest. Note the damage here: the club was longer, extended to the left, and was held in both hands. The wild man is sometimes shown riding a lion, symbolising Man in control of the King of Beasts. His hairiness is frequently emphasised and this may hark back to the contrast between the smooth Jacob and the hairy Esau in Genesis ch.27.

The wild man was popular in coats-of-arms as a fertility mascot. The Wood family coat of arms, with three wild men of the woods with clubs, occurs several times in the Cathedral; for example, in the window immediately south of the great east window and also in the library east window.

N.17 *(The Mayor's Stall) – A griffin with rabbits*

The evil griffin attacks the rabbit warren and catches a rabbit while another rabbit escapes down a hole. The victim has not time to think and is clearly the unlucky one whose time has come. Even so, it may be that a sacrifice theme was being considered here. Jesus said: *Greater Love has no Man than this, that he lays down his life for his friends* (John ch.15 v.13). By giving his life, the caught rabbit gave the escaping rabbit the chance to get to safety. Sometimes used as a symbol of innocence, a rabbit's only defence against such an attack is

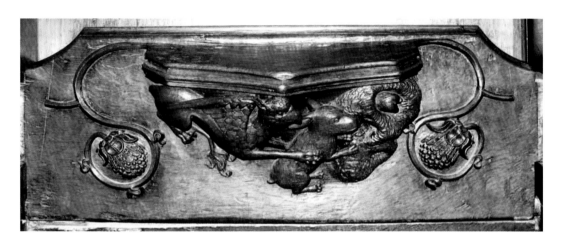

rapid flight.

It may also be that this gave the carvers the chance to show wit and humour, all the better if the joke took the traditional form of turning things upside down. Eighteenth century Chap Books included numerous examples, such as two men pulling a plough guided by an ox, an ox killing the butcher or the fish catching the anglers. 'Putting the cart before the horse' appears on a Beverley misericord and a number have survived depicting women beating their husbands. The less powerful getting 'one-up' on the more powerful was a very popular inversion. A classic example from the fifteenth century appears in an engraving by Israel von Meckenen, copied in the Rabbits' Revenge misericord at Manchester, where the rabbits turn the spit on which the hunter is roasting, while other rabbits tend the cooking pots[32].

Charles Dodgson (Lewis Carroll) visited Ripon cathedral many times in the years before he wrote *Alice in Wonderland*. His father was a residentiary canon and his name can be found on the canons' board in the south-west tower. The rabbit going down the hole could well have inspired Lewis Carroll as the opening of the fantasy, published in 1865. Other Lewis Carroll connections are described in a booklet available in the Cathedral shop.

To conclude

At various times some repairs to the choir stalls and related carvings have had to be undertaken. This included misericords S.16, which is an 1860s creation, and S.1, which was very extensively restored by Scott at the same time.

Having said that, we have in Ripon a quite superb set of thirty-four misericords, most done by a famous 'school' of woodcarvers well over five hundred years ago. It set a new, very high standard for the region – and beyond.

Other Interesting Carvings

Protruding Tongues

[Sketch from the undated *Symbolism in Ripon Cathedral*, Ripon Cathedral, c.1975]

Heads with protruding tongues are found in lots of churches, and are sometimes regarded as derisory images. Three carved stone heads, one with a protruding tongue, can easily be picked out in the choir at Ripon (left). There are others carved in wood on the choir stalls and screens.

At Ripon, there are also lions' heads with protruding tongues as supporters on the misericord of the pelican in her piety (detail from misericord S.13). There is debate about the meaning of this symbol.

The Pomegranate

The pomegranate, a heraldic device of the house of Aragon, was usually depicted with seeds showing through a split skin. It was regarded as a Resurrection symbol by the Christian church, and one was often shown held by the Christ-child. It fell out of use in England after the twelfth century, although the plant could be grown and the fruit imported.

Charles Tracy has found pomegranates in woodcarvings at Windsor (1480), Ripon (1490), St David's and Tong (c.1500).

Man Exposing Himself

This carving is hidden in the North return stalls and we cannot be sure the stallholder knew of his existence. Was the man urinating on the cleric below? It is the sole example in Ripon of a scatological carving. In medieval churches such images occasionally survived attempts by Puritans and Victorians to eliminate them (see p.14).

Poppyheads

Some of the most striking features of the woodwork at Ripon are the poppyheads, or finials, which climax the bench ends. Their name is a corruption of the French *poupée*, a doll. Amongst them is what is known as the *Aysgarth flower*, which can be seen on the mayor's bench end (right). It was used at times as an identifying feature of the Ripon carvers.

Crowned Triple Head

The triple head is mounted above the archway leading from the choir to the nave. It has four eyes, three noses and three mouths and is well formed. With its crown and natural detailing, it is similar to the head of an angel on one of the misericords and to a corbel head stop on the backing of the north return stalls. Three faces in one head has obvious connotations with the Trinity. It can also be interpreted as a Janus head, or as Past, Present, and Future.

Beaver

In the lower canopy just above misericord S.11 is another carved creature. It can be found about 80cm above the capping, against the glass. It used to be seen as a dog chasing its tail, but now with the tail being so flat is thought to be a beaver. This is possibly an 1860s carving.

Bestiaries[33] tell us that hunters pursued a beaver to obtain, not its fur, but its testicles (used in medicinal preparations). When about to be caught, the beaver, knowing this (*how?*), bites off its testicles, drops them for the hunter to see, then makes its escape. Small wonder the beaver became extinct in our region!

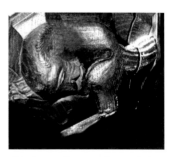

The beaver is not easily seen in its entirety as it wraps around a column head. This is a composite of three images.

Demons

The elbow between misericords N.9 and N.10 bears these two demons which are unlike any others at Ripon.

Ceiling Bosses

During the 1860s Scott restored the ceilings in both the Nave and the Choir. Bosses of much earlier date were re-incorporated into the structure of the Choir ceiling, whereas the Nave had all-new bosses made in a medieval style. Traditionally, these have been called roof bosses but since there is a large space between the actual roof and Scott's ceiling we feel that ceiling bosses is a more appropriate term. The scar of an earlier ceiling can be seen on the east wall of the Choir, immediately above the apex of the window stonework.

Over the years there has been much debate as to whether the bosses are from the original 1180s building; or from the 1280s reconstruction following the collapse of the east end; or from the 1480s rebuild after the partial collapse of the Central Tower. In the last case they would be contemporary with the misericords and other sections that survived the 1660 fall of the Spire. It is generally believed that most of them are much older than the repairs after the 1660 damage or the subsequent restoration by Blore in the 19th century (when they are known to be younger in origin this is pointed out in the descriptions below).

The main sources of this information are Hallett[34], Forster[35] and Parker[36], but we include some other ideas.

The bosses are larger than they may appear from the choir floor; some of the figures are about 5 feet (1.5 metres) tall.

In total, there are thirteen gilded bosses along the length of the choir ceiling; they are numbered here from east to west.

An image of each of the thirteen bosses is shown in the boxes on the following pages. The text offers an explanation for each of them.

Numbering of Choir Ceiling Bosses

13 12 11 10 9 8 7 6 5 4 3 2 1

West end   East end

| Boss 1 | Boss 2 | Boss 3 |

<u>Boss 1</u>: a head - as it is in prime position, i.e. the east end, it could represent God the Father (compare Boss 11).

<u>Boss 2</u>: generally thought to be The Good Samaritan story. Certainly the naked man is being assisted by the other who is fully clothed, which fits the details of our Lord's parable (Luke ch.10 v.29-37). Parker describes this boss as: *a holy person relieving a distressed person*[37].

Another possibility, based on the similarity between the naked man and Adam in Boss 3, is that this shows God the Father placing Adam in the Garden of Eden. Alternatively, it could be a reference to our Lord's injunction on his followers to carry out acts of charity unstintingly and joyfully. Clothing the naked was seen in medieval times as one of the seven acts of Christian charity or mercy (Matthew ch.25 v.31-46). The Gospel quotes six acts of mercy:

- feeding the hungry
- giving drink to the thirsty
- clothing the naked
- giving shelter to strangers
- visiting the sick
- visiting those in prison.

    In later centuries burying the dead was added.

An 1860s window in the west wall of the north transept (one of the Staveley windows) shows Matthew's original six acts of mercy. A 1420s example of all seven can be seen in a window at All Saints' Church, North Street, York.

<u>Boss 3</u>: the expulsion from Paradise. Adam and Eve flee from the sword-wielding Angel. Note the city-style gate in the wall around the Garden of Eden, perhaps reflecting the medieval thinking that the City was a place of freedom and opportunity, while the Countryside was a place of servitude.

Boss 4: the Annunciation – note the vase with a lily between Mary and the Archangel Gabriel – a white flower (fleur de lys) especially associated with Mary and with purity. This boss was partially restored by Scott – an early photograph clearly shows both figures have different faces[38].

Boss 5: the crucifixion – with St John and the Blessed Virgin on either side of the dying Christ. [This scene was carved by one of Scott's woodcarvers in the 1860s]. It is a second example of the scene in St John's gospel, which would also have been seen atop the Rood beam between the Nave and the Crossing until the Reformation. This is the only boss with a significant area of colour other than gold: in this case, blue of the shade associated with Mary – though it may have faded somewhat.

Boss 6: a bishop and a king enthroned side-by-side. The bishop wears a mitre and the king a crown (cf. Boss 8). This may illustrate the medieval ideal of the close working-together of the divine and wordly authorities.

Boss 7: a bishop enthroned, giving a blessing. This is very similar to the adjacent Boss 8.

Boss 8: a king(?) enthroned, but apparently not crowned. This may be Christ in Majesty blessing the world – though it might be expected that He would wear a crown or a halo (cf. Boss 11).

Boss 9: a bishop, standing among trees, giving the blessing.

Boss 10: a man leading a (naked?) woman to a church door – this could be part of the medieval wedding ritual. Parker has: *a holy person bringing a mendicant to the porch of the church*[39].

Boss 11: a head, possibly meant to be our Lord Jesus, but again with no crown or halo.

Boss 12: an angel seated on a throne with foliage beneath – a larger boss than the others.

Boss 13: a head with very odd ears. There are some similarities to the Green Man of Misericord N.15, e.g. the pointed ears and the fringe, but the Green Man has vegetation coming from his mouth while the boss has a protruding tongue.

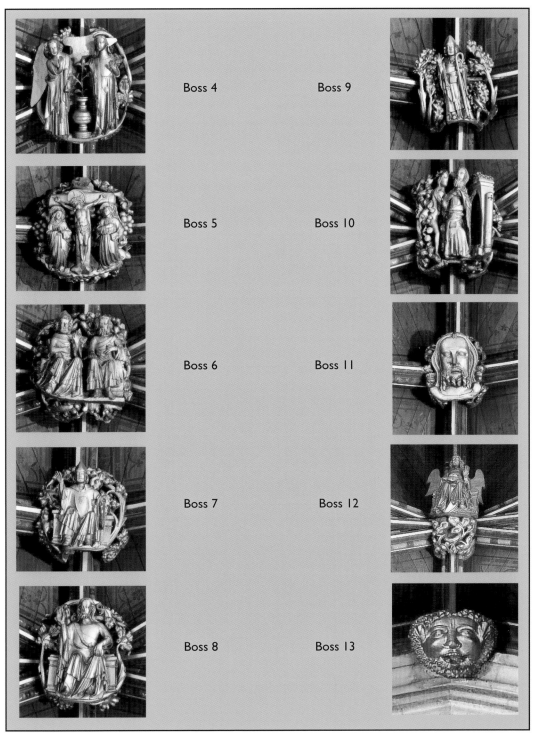

Boss 4

Boss 9

Boss 5

Boss 10

Boss 6

Boss 11

Boss 7

Boss 12

Boss 8

Boss 13

Victorian Choir Screens

The carved wooden screens dividing off the Choir from the North and South Aisles are all features added by Sir George Gilbert Scott in the 1860s renovation. Parts of earlier screens do appear to be incorporated, notably in the screen nearest to the Bishop's Stall.

The screen dividing the North Choir Aisle into two was erected sometime around the turn of the 20th century. As it was made by a group of lady carvers it is sometimes referred to as 'the Ladies' Screen'. The west face of the beam states: *Sancti Wilfridi Capella* (the Chapel of St Wilfrid).

Modern Misericord

In 2003 a new misericord was designed by Brian Partridge of York and carved by Graham Gamble of Acaster Malbis. This is an excellent replica of the griffin and rabbit misericord but with the addition of Alice of *Alice's Adventures in Wonderland* riding the griffin, together with the rocking-horse fly, the White Rabbit watch and a string of flowers. This modern misericord was carved for the exhibition at Thorpe Prebend House – the Ripon Cathedral Heritage Centre in High St. Agnesgate, close to the Cathedral.

Photograph by M.H. Taylor

Closing Thoughts on the Medieval Carvers

Did the same carvers work in Manchester and Beverley?

Let us now attempt to sum up the position of the Ripon woodcarvings and their supposed links with Manchester and Beverley. Canon Purvis argued that the output was possible through a standardisation of parts.

Charles Tracy and Christa Grössinger are the currently published authorities in the field.

Tracy's views may perhaps be summarised as follows:

- He claims there is no documentary evidence of Bromflet working in Manchester or Beverley and that it was too difficult for the carvers to cope with all the work at the same time.

- He measured and found non-standardised components. He regards none of Purvis's specific motival comparisons between Ripon and Manchester (vine scrolls, oak leaves, Ripon amphisbena as sufficiently convincing.

- He also dismisses pellet, scallop and brattish ornament as not stylistically diagnostic.

- He recognised no very close iconographical or stylistic connections between Ripon, Beverley and Manchester, but found that the three fit into a category of development and influence which began at Ripon.

- He considers that the work of the Ripon woodcarvers stands at the beginning of a new style in the North, equal to anything in the country of its date.

- Despite the lack of documentary evidence, William Bromflet may have been loaned to Manchester and a Ripon carver may have worked there.

- In his opinion, Ripon should not be denigrated because of subsequent developments at Manchester and Beverley, but the work of its carvers should be acknowledged as setting an exciting new style.

Dr Grössinger, while initially accepting Canon Purvis's work, later moved towards Dr Tracy's position.

Dimensions of Choir Stall seats

Regarding the possible standardisation of wooden components, the choir seat tops were measured during the preparation of this book. Their individual widths and depths are shown in the Appendix on page 64. The graphical representation of these rather variable dimensions seems to indicate little in the way of standardisation.

A Final Word

Whatever the actual rôle of the Ripon carvers throughout the north of England, their work is clearly something to be treasured and protected.

Anyone interested in finding out more about this subject is recommended to read the works of Francis Bond, Canon Purvis, Charles Tracy and Christa Grössinger. These are listed in the Bibliography on page 67.

Appendix

Centre dimensions of Choir Stall seats above each misericord

Number	SOUTH-side Misericord Subject	Depth, cm	Width, cm
S.1	C19th Angel	27.4	82.7
S.2	Angel with dated shield	26.6	72.4
S.3	Lion and winged animal	27.3	67.3
S.4	Grifffin with human leg	26.7	72.4
S.5	Owl	31.2	62.7
S.6	Mermaid	30.4	64.3
S.7	Pig playing bagpipes	30.5	62.8
S.8	Jonah cast overboard	31.2	62.6
S.9	Man pushing woman in cart	30.7	60.1
S.10	Fox and goose	30.1	63.7
S.11	Griffin	29.4	63.8
S.12	Antelope gorged and chained	30.1	62.6
S.13	Pelican in her piety	30.1	66.4
S.14	Jonah cast ashore	29.7	64.0
S.15	Samson and the gates of Gaza	31.2	64.1
S.16	C19th head	29.0	66.8
S.17	Spies of Eschol	30.6	74.8
Number	**NORTH-side Misericord Subject**	**Depth, cm**	**Width, cm**
N.1	Lion with upturned head	30.5	81.5
N.2	Wyvern & dogs	30.4	76.3
N.3	Angel & shield	29.6	76.5
N.4	Wyvern & birds	26.8	71.2
N.5	Foliage	30.6	64.4
N.6	Flowers & foliage	30.7	61.9
N.7	Lion & monkey	30.6	62.7
N.8	Vine with grapes	30.6	59.9
N.9	Two birds eating fruit	30.3	62.3
N.10	Two antelope resting	30.4	64.7
N.11	Fox preaching to cock & goose	29.5	62.0
N.12	Fox & two geese	30.4	63.1
N.13	Fox & two dogs	30.3	62.4
N.14	Two dragons fighting	30.7	63.0
N.15	Green man upside down	29.4	63.0
N.16	Wild man	30.5	66.2
N.17	Griffin holding rabbit	30.6	77.2

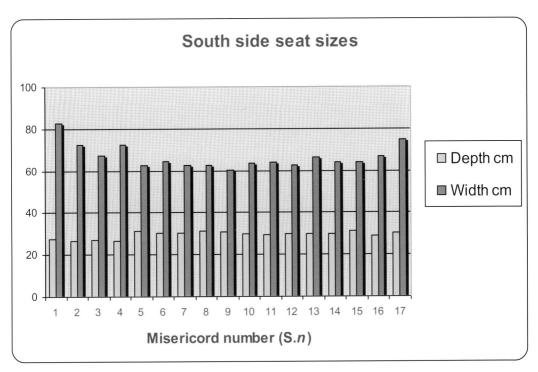

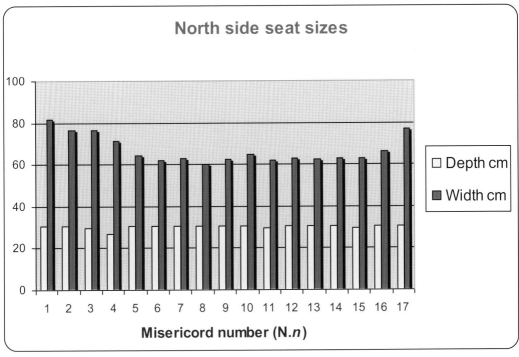

References from text

Full details of sources are given in the Bibliography table opposite

1	Grössinger, C. (1997), p.11.
2	Tracy, C. (1990), p.19.
3	Grössinger, C. (2002), p.34.
4	Pacey, A. (2005), private correspondence.
5	Forster, W. et al (1993), p.82.
6	Tracy, C. (1990), pp.19-20.
7	See the works of Revd Hudson and Canon Purvis.
8	Tracy, C. (1990), p.26.
9	Thanks to Janet Walker for bringing this to our attention.
10	Jones, M. (2000), p.159.
11	Grössinger, C. (1997), p.21.
12	Tracy, C. (1990), p.26.
13	Hallett, C. 1901), p.108.
14	Tracy, C. (1990), p.18.
15	Brewer (1870), p.29.
16	Anon. (c.1908), p.165.
17	Grössinger, C. (1997), p.11.
18	Bond, F. (1910), ch.XXXI.
19	Tracy, C. (2008), private communication.
20	Rickman, T. (1881), p.307.
21	Grössinger, C. (1997), p.66.
22	Grössinger, C. (2005), personal communication.
23	Smith, L. (1914), p.125.
24	Rickman, T. (1881), pp.297-8.
25	Webb, D. (2000), pp.79-80.
26	Grössinger, C. (1997), p.17.
27	Barber, R., tr. (1992), p.26.
28	Grössinger, C. (1989), p.13.
29	Grössinger, C. (1989), p.15.
30	Friar, S. (1996), p.328.
31	Frewins, C. (2005), p.155.
32	Bond, F. (1910), ch.XXIV.
33	Barber, R., tr. (1992), pp.43-4.
34	Hallett, C. (1901), p.103.
35	Forster, W. et al (1993), p.102.
36	Parker, G. (1902), pp.83-4.
37	Parker, G. (1902), p.84.
38	Forster, W. et al (1993), p.102.
39	Parker, G. (1902), p.84.

Bibliography

Anderson, M.D. (1971), *History and Imagery in British Churches*, London: John Murray Publishers.

Anderson, M.D. (1954), *Misericords*, London: Penguin Books.

Anon. (c.1908), *Historic Ripon*, Ripon: Taylor (printer), p.165.

Barber, R., tr .(1992), *Bestiary*, London: Folio Society, [paperback edn(1999), Woodbridge: The Boydell Press].

Bond, Francis (1910), *Woodcarvings in English Churches - I Misericords*, London: Henry Frowde.

Brewer, E.C. (1870), *Dictionary of Phrase and Fable*, (e.g. 14th Edition, 1989, London: Cassell & Co.).

Forster, W., **Robson**, W., **Deadman**, J. (1993), *Ripon Cathedral – Its History and Architecture*, York: William Sessions.

Frewins, Clive (2005), *The Church Explorer's Handbook*, Norwich: Canterbury Press.

Friar, Stephen (1996), *A Companion to the English Parish Church*, Stroud: Sutton Publishing.

Grössinger, Christa (2002), 'The Relationship Between Manchester Cathedral Misericords and Those at Ripon Cathedral and Beverley Minster', *Transactions of Lancashire & Cheshire Antiquarian Society*, Vol. 98, Manchester.

Grössinger, Christa (1989), *Ripon Cathedral Misericords - 500 Years Anniversary*, Ripon : Dean and Chapter Ripon Cathedral.

Grössinger, Christa (1997), *The World Upside Down*, London: Harvey Miller.

Hallett, Cecil (1901), *Ripon – The Cathedral and See*, London: George Bell & Sons.

Harrison, Lynn (c. 1980), *The Ripon Misericords and Choir Stalls*, Illus. Jennifer Deadman, Ripon: Ripon Cathedral.

Hudson, Rev. H.A. (1924), *The Medieval Woodwork of Manchester Cathedral*, Manchester: Sherratt & Hughes.

Jones, M. (2000), in *Beverley Minster an Illustrated History*, ed. R. Horrocks, Beverley: Friends of Beverley Minster.

Laird, Marshall (1986), *English Misericords*, London: John Murray Publishers.

Parker, G. (1902), *Ripon Cathedral Past and Present*, Ripon: George Parker.

Purvis, Canon J.S. (1929), 'The Ripon Carvers and the Lost Choir-Stalls of Bridlington Priory' *Yorkshire Archaeological Journal*, Vol. XXIX, Leeds: Yorkshire Archaeological Society.

Purvis, Canon J.S. (1936), 'Use of Continental woodcuts and prints by the "Ripon School" of Woodcarvers in the early sixteenth century', London: Society of Antiquaries.

Remnant, G.L. (1969), *A catalogue of Misericords in Great Britain*, Oxford: Oxford University Press.

Rickman, Thomas (1881), *Gothic Architecture*, Oxford: Parker & Co.

Smith, J.C.D. (1974), *A Guide to Church Woodcarvings: Misericords and Bench Ends*, Newton Abbot: David and Charles.

Smith, Lucius (1914), *The Story of Ripon Minster*, Leeds: Richard Jackson, p.125.

Tracy, Charles (1990), *English Gothic Choir Stalls 1400-1550*, Woodbridge: The Boydell Press.

Tracy, Charles (1985), 'Dating the Misericords from the Thirteenth Century Choir Stalls at Exeter Cathedral', in *Medieval Art and Architecture at Exeter Cathedral (ed. F. Kelly)*, British Archeological Association Conference Transactions, Leeds: Maney Publishing.

Webb, Diana (2000), *Pilgrimage in Medieval England*, London: Hambledon and London.

Index

Numbers in **bold** show pages on which there are illustrations